EMPOWER YOURSELF

Daily Affirmations to Reclaim Your Power!

MIRANDA KERR

HAY
HOUSE

HAY HOUSE, INC.
Carlsbad, California • New York City
London • Sydney • Johannesburg
Vancouver • Hong Kong • New Delhi

Copyright © 2013 by Hay House Pty Ltd

Published and distributed in the United States by: Hay House, Inc.: www.hayhouse.com®
• **Published and distributed in Australia by:** Hay House Australia Pty. Ltd.: www.hayhouse
.com.au • **Published and distributed in the United Kingdom by:** Hay House UK, Ltd.:
www.hayhouse.co.uk • **Published and distributed in the Republic of South Africa by:**
Hay House SA (Pty), Ltd.: www.hayhouse.co.za • **Distributed in Canada by:** Raincoast
Books: www.raincoast.com • **Published in India by:** Hay House Publishers India:
www.hayhouse.co.in

Illustrations by Dwayne Labbe
Design by Rhett Nacson
Typeset by Simon Patterson Bookhouse
Edited by Margie Tubbs

The author of this book does not dispense medical advice nor prescribe the use of any technique
as a form of treatment for physical or medical problems without the advice of a physician, either
directly or indirectly. The intent of the author is only to offer information of a general nature to help
you in your quest for physical fitness and good health. In the event you use any of the information in
this book for yourself, the author and the publisher assume no responsibility for your actions.

Library of Congress Control Number: 2014942510

ISBN: 978-1-4019-4633-3

10 9 8 7 6 5 4 3 2
1st edition, September 2014

This book is dedicated to Flynn,
who has started his journey
to true empowerment.

Dear Friends,

Thank you for joining me on this journey to true empowerment! I am so happy to share my thoughts and philosophy with you.

For many years now, I have traveled around the world as a model, commercial spokesperson, author, and advocate for numerous causes involving animals, the environment, and children. I couldn't have done any of this without genuine self-worth and personal power.

The truth of the matter is, I wasn't *born* a strong and confident woman . . . I became one through my own efforts to cultivate these attributes daily. My dedication to a daily practice of yoga, prayer, and meditation, along with my commitment to a healthy diet, are an integral part of my success. In addition I have found that by focusing on the positive, trusting my inner guidance, and having faith, I can overcome fear and doubt and manifest my dreams into reality.

And that is what I desire for *you!* I want you to visualize what you want, be absolutely certain that you can achieve it, and use this book as a tool to help you manifest it. The more you manifest your dreams into reality, the more you can be an inspiration and a shining light for others on this glorious planet so they can follow your lead. I wholeheartedly believe that it is the responsibility of each one of us to bring peace and harmony to our *own* lives . . . then and only then will we bring peace to the world.

A lot has happened in my life since *Treasure Yourself* was published. As a first-time author, I have been delighted to hear from readers who enjoyed my book, and to hear that it provided them inspiration in a variety of ways. While I was writing it, it was my hope that sharing my story would help others. I am both humbled and grateful to discover that this has come true.

I am thankful that new experiences and opportunities continue to arise in many areas of my life. Apart from allocating more time to writing, I'm also continuing to build my career both as a model and businesswoman.

Of course, the most significant change in my life recently has been becoming a mother. Flynn has brought a new level of perspective to my life, and I feel thoroughly blessed. I was fortunate to grow up in a wonderful, loving family, and I'm grateful for my close relationships with my parents, brother, grandparents, and extended family. I am delighted to build a similar, nurturing family environment for Flynn.

Having Flynn in my life has made me realize how easy it is to get distracted by all the activities that demand my time and, as a consequence, miss what is most important. I used to think that if I took time to slow down and relax that I was being lazy, but Flynn has taught me that the moments that really make up a life are those quiet, peaceful ones with those you love. I know now it is essential to relax and be present. In my busy life, the times I value most are when I slow down to read to Flynn, bathe him, share meals with him, or just play in the garden with him.

I've also learned some other very important lessons that I'd like to share with you.

I've learned to keep my life in balance. With so much going on in our lives, and so many different priorities, it is easy to get out of balance. Placing too much emphasis on any one area of our lives, be it work, family, friends, health, romance, or spirituality, can leave us feeling strained and depleted. I notice that when each aspect of my life is balanced with the others, I really perform at my best. My personal goal is to be balanced, thoughtful, heart-centered, and relaxed as much as possible. When I am able to do this, I feel a sense of harmony flowing throughout my life.

I've learned through experience to be very discerning about where I focus my energy and attention. I believe that when you focus your attention on your goals, you can achieve whatever you desire. It is really important that we each focus on the things in life that matter most to us!

I've learned to keep the discipline of thinking positive thoughts and saying positive things about others. We are fortunate to live in an age where technology is developing at an amazing rate, allowing us to connect with each other in ways that weren't possible before. This is a wonderful thing because people who can't physically connect can still stay in touch. Yet it can also bring with it a set of challenges, such as the possibility of unkind or untrue comments spreading around the globe in an instant. My experience has taught me that when I stay positive, I attract positivity in return.

I've learned to avoid taking things personally and not concern myself with the opinions of those who don't truly know me. Let's remind ourselves to appreciate our uniqueness, so we feel free to be ourselves.

I've learned to appreciate the unique talents of others as well as my own. I find that when I recognize and appreciate the talents of others, I am able to forge positive relationships where we can all benefit from one another. No matter what our specific talents are, the important thing is to acknowledge that we all have unique skills and strengths to share.

I've learned to ask for help, which used to be difficult for me. Being human is about reciprocity, giving and receiving. There are times in life when we will need assistance from others and times when we will be asked to give support to others. It's easier for me to ask for help now, because I am in turn committed to giving it to others. The more we give, the more we open ourselves to receive.

I ask that as you read the words in this book, you give each thought, practical suggestion, and affirmation your focused attention . . . and intention. Some of what I've written might seem obvious—that is, common-sense advice on eating right, being a good person, and so on—but sometimes the ideas that impact people the most are the ones that are the simplest. I tried to present them in a way that doesn't "tell" you what to do, but merely reaffirms what you consciously or subconsciously already know is appropriate and true for you.

My hope is that you will not just quickly read each statement and affirmation and then dismiss it, but actually make a concerted effort to apply what you've read to everyday situations. You can read the entries in order or open the book spontaneously. If you do the latter, you might very well find that the page you turn to contains information that is exactly right for you on that particular day.

I truly believe in what I've written within these pages. These concepts, which I hope I have presented in a straightforward and meaningful way, have enhanced my life and helped make me the woman I am today. Now that I am the proud mother of a precious little boy, I feel more compelled than ever to be a positive influence in the world.

Basically, I wrote this book for *you* . . . the daughter, the son, the sister, the brother, the mother, the father, the wife, the husband, the partner, the friend. I wrote it for those of you who have already found your place in this world, and for those still on the journey to figuring out who you really are. I wrote it for those of you who may have lost your way . . . but are on the road to finding yourself again.

I wish all of you the best in life: ease, health, contentment, success, prosperity, love, joy, peace, and the manifestation of your dreams. Remember, to *feel* the best and *be* the best you have to *do* your best . . . and the first step on that path is to . . . ***Empower Yourself!***

Much love,
Miranda
xxx

Behind the scenes of the
2012 Victoria's Secret Fashion Show.

I was so proud to be named
Kids Helpline Ambassador.

━━━━◆◆◆━━━━

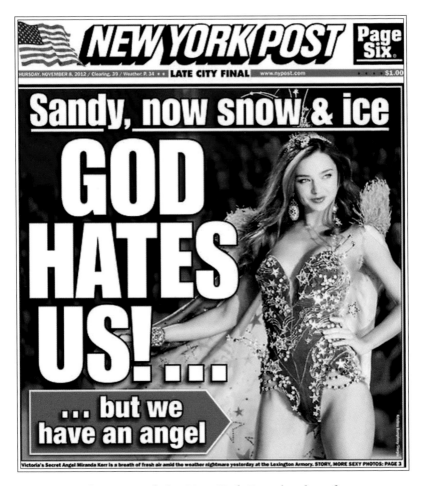

The cover of the *New York Post* the day after
the Victoria's Secret fashion show.

Being flexible is a strength.
Reebok Satisfaction Campaign.

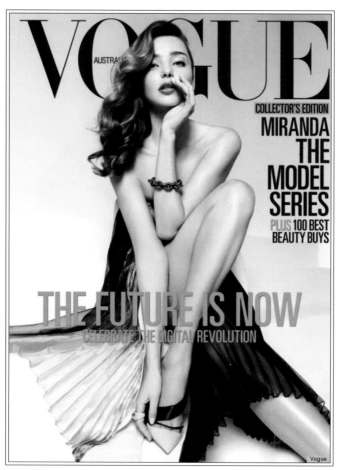

One of my recent covers for Australian *Vogue*.

A shot Orlando took of me in New Zealand.

Love to stretch it out! British *Vogue*.

Kisses! Love, Miranda *xxx*

Australia Day Issue of *Grazia* Australia.

On the cover of *Purple Fashion*.

Behind the scenes for Victoria's Secret.

Harper's Bazaar Australia.

When you Empower Yourself, you . . .

RESPECT WHO YOU ARE

You respect yourself in every area of your life . . .
at school, at home, at work, and in your interpersonal
relationships. You do not allow anyone to speak to you
in an abusive fashion or to undermine you in any way.
You surround yourself with positive, loving,
supportive individuals.

Empowering Affirmation . . .

I respect myself every day, in every way.

ASK FOR HELP WHEN YOU NEED IT

There are times in your life when you really
need assistance from friends, relatives,
mentors, and health professionals. You feel
free to ask for help. You know that it's a sign
of strength, not weakness, to do so. You realize
that we are all here to help each other.

Empowering Affirmation . . .

I ask for help when I need it, and
my life improves as a result.

APPRECIATE EACH DAY

You wake up each morning feeling appreciative
for another day on Earth. Your heart is
full of gratitude. You do your best to take
nothing for granted and make the most
of every second, minute, and hour.

Empowering Affirmation . . .

My heart is filled with gratitude every
day that I live on this wonderful planet.
With every breath, I celebrate life.

VOLUNTEER WHENEVER
AND WHEREVER YOU CAN

I am a channel for Divine energy. I donate money
to those in need, I volunteer when I can, and
I visit children's hospitals or homes for the elderly
and spend time connecting with people. I look for
creative ways to help, uplift, and inspire others.

Empowering Affirmation . . .

**I volunteer whenever I can and help
make the world a better place.**

CONTINUE YOUR EDUCATION REGARDLESS OF AGE

You take classes, read books and magazines of all kinds, go to lectures, surf the Internet, and have stimulating discussions with knowledgeable people.

Empowering Affirmation . . .

I continue my education throughout my life. I am so happy to expand and grow.

EXPRESS YOUR CREATIVITY

You release your creativity by writing, singing,
dancing, playing an instrument, taking
photographs, painting, sculpting . . .
whatever it is that helps you express
yourself. You have so much to give!

Empowering Affirmation . . .

My creativity is limitless. I let it flow and
open up the right side of my brain.

LOOK YOUR BEST

You wear clothes that are flattering to
your individual body shape, and you
make sure that your hair and makeup
(if you wear any) complement your
overall look. You accentuate your positive
attributes, and your confidence shows.

Empowering Affirmation . . .

I am beautiful inside and out, and
my inner radiance shines.

HANDLE YOUR MONEY WITH CARE

You work hard for the money you make; so you
save, invest, and spend with care. You make
provisions for emergencies and also set aside
funds for vacations and charitable giving.

Empowering Affirmation . . .

I spend wisely, give generously to charity,
and live within my means.

When you **Empower Yourself***, you* . . .

NURTURE YOUR FRIENDSHIPS

Your friendships with others are characterized by respect, love, and laughter. You listen when your friends need an ear; you are supportive and you share the details of your life with empathy, understanding, and compassion.

Empowering Affirmation . . .

I am the type of friend to others
that I want them to be to me.

MAKE EXERCISE A PART OF YOUR DAILY ROUTINE

You walk, go to the gym, play tennis, do yoga, swim, take an exercise class . . . or just take the stairs instead of the elevator. You don't let a day go by without doing some form of physical activity that you enjoy.

Empowering Affirmation . . .

I get my blood flowing each day, and it feels so good!

When you **Empower Yourself**, *you . . .*

TAKE A STAND FOR WHAT YOU BELIEVE IN

You have your own opinions about life. You express them with tact and diplomacy.

Empowering Affirmation . . .

My opinions count; I express them openly and respectfully.

HONOR YOUR SEXUALITY

You are a loving person filled with passion
and a healthy desire for sex, but you don't feel
pressured to be intimate. You seek committed
relationships and also protect yourself at all times.

Empowering Affirmation . . .

I love myself and my body, so when
the time is right to have a sexual
relationship, I engage in safe practices.

VALUE THE ELDERS IN YOUR LIFE

Senior citizens are part of your life every
day, so you make a point of spending time
with them whenever you can. Whether they
are friends, relatives, or just strangers you
happen to encounter, they have so much
to teach you and so much love to give.

Empowering Affirmation . . .

**I am kind, respectful, and attentive
to the elders in my life.**

READ BOOKS AND VIEW MOVIES THAT NOURISH YOUR SOUL

You have so many choices with respect to reading material and films; so you choose the books and movies that uplift you, rather than those that bring you down. It's your choice!

Empowering Affirmation . . .

I choose to read books and view movies that enrich my life.

USE THE INTERNET WITH CARE

You shop, date, and do so many other things on the Internet; but you are very careful when you do so. You protect your identity, avoid questionable websites, and do research before sending your credit-card or other personal data to anyone.

Empowering Affirmation . . .

I am vigilant when doing things online.

REVEL IN THE JOYS OF NATURE

You are a huge fan of Mother Nature,
and you are in awe of her wondrous gifts.
You respect every blade of grass, every
babbling brook, every tree and flower . . .
and you soak up all of nature's goodness!

Empowering Affirmation . . .

I go outside in nature every day and
embrace the wonders that surround me.
I am so grateful for our glorious planet.

PRACTICE SPIRITUAL AND RELIGIOUS TOLERANCE

You may have strong religious convictions, or you may be someone who is spiritual without being religious—or perhaps you are an atheist or an agnostic. Whatever the case, you accept that there is room for multiple viewpoints.

Empowering Affirmation . . .

I respect others' views on spirituality and religion, and they respect mine as well.

SHOW RESPECT WHEN USING MODERN TECHNOLOGY

You appreciate the may technological advances that are available to you, such as cell phones, MP3 players, ebook readers, and other modern devices; and you make a point of being polite when using them in public.

Empowering Affirmation . . .

I appreciate the ways in which technology has made my life easier, and I am respectful whenever I use these devices.

ARE PUNCTUAL

You honor your own time as well as
that of others, so you make sure you
are not late for engagements.

Empowering Affirmation . . .

I plan wisely so that I am on time for
dates, meetings, and appointments.

USE WORDS CAREFULLY

You think twice before you speak, write, or send an e-mail. Your words have so much power . . . and once they're out there, they can't be taken back.

Empowering Affirmation . . .

I take the feelings of others into consideration.
I appreciate the power of my words, and I
choose to use them in a positive way.

MAKE GRATITUDE A WAY OF LIFE

You go about your day expressing gratitude
for everything you have and everything
you are. You say "thank you" once more
before you fall asleep at night.

Empowering Affirmation . . .

I am grateful for everybody and everything
in my life! I am so blessed with abundance,
joy, health, and contentment.

CHOOSE A CAREER THAT BRINGS YOU JOY

Your profession stimulates you. You don't just work for the money, you work for the satisfaction your career gives you; so you choose a job that brings you fulfillment.

Empowering Affirmation ...

I choose a profession that fulfills me.
I enjoy going to work, and others
enjoy working with me.

TELL THE TRUTH

You speak your truth with your friends, your
family, your co-workers, your neighbors, and
anyone else you come in contact with.

Empowering Affirmation . . .

I am honest with others, as well as myself.

TAKE CARE OF YOUR DENTAL HEALTH

You brush your teeth at least twice a day, floss after you eat, and see a dentist twice a year for checkups. Your smile is one of the first things people notice about you, so you want your teeth to be clean and fresh at all times.

Empowering Affirmation . . .

I practice good oral hygiene on a daily basis, and smile often.

EAT SLOWLY AND MINDFULLY

Whether you are sitting down for a four-course meal in a restaurant or just eating at your desk, you take the time to appreciate the food you are eating and savor every bite.

Empowering Affirmation . . .

I eat with gratitude and mindfulness.

KEEP CONFIDENCES

When someone asks you to keep a secret, you do
so, knowing that you will not betray this promise.
You expect others to show you the same respect.

Empowering Affirmation . . .

**I keep confidences, and
others keep mine in turn.**

LEAVE YOUR EGO AT THE DOOR

You realize that letting your ego get out of hand can have a negative effect on your relationships, your work, and your overall life. You keep it in check and find that everything goes much more smoothly.

Empowering Affirmation . . .

I relinquish my ego and live humbly and appreciatively.

MENTOR OTHERS

You offer to be a mentor to younger people—
or anyone of any age—who can benefit from
your knowledge and experience. You make the
time to do so and feel good about doing it.

Empowering Affirmation . . .

I take the time to be a mentor, and everyone
involved benefits from the experience.

ASK SOMEONE TO MENTOR *YOU*

You seek out an older person whom you respect
and ask that he or she mentor you. This person
teaches you, advises you, and serves as an
example, both personally and professionally.

Empowering Affirmation . . .

I find a mentor who can stimulate
and encourage my personal and
professional growth.

PLAN YOUR DAY WITH CARE

You don't run around aimlessly. While you
do your errands, go about your workday, or
deal with your family, you plan ahead so
you can complete your tasks at leisure.

Empowering Affirmation . . .

I plan my day in a way that flows.

CLEAN OUT YOUR CLOSETS

You feel better when you clear the clutter in
your life, so you clean out your closets and
donate the clothes, shoes, and other items
you no longer use to a worthy cause.

Empowering Affirmation . . .

I clean out my closets regularly and
give away what I no longer have a need for.

PAY YOUR TAXES

You pay what is due when it comes to your
taxes, as you know that the revenue they
generate contributes to needed public services.
You are honest and forthcoming when filling
out tax forms, and you file them on time.

Empowering Affirmation . . .

I pay the taxes that are required of
me promptly and accurately.

RESEARCH YOUR FAMILY HISTORY

You ask your older relatives about the history of
your family, or do research on the Internet to
find out as much as possible about your lineage.
You learn much about yourself in the process.

Empowering Affirmation . . .

I look into my family history as a way
of finding out more about myself.
I expand and grow from this process.

LIVE WITHOUT REGRET

You go through many experiences in your life—some joyful, some painful, some confusing—but no matter what happens, you regret nothing. Everything you go through teaches you a valuable lesson. You have the choice to live from fear or love.

Empowering Affirmation . . .

I accept the value of every experience, and live my life fearlessly and with love.

REMEMBER BIRTHDAYS
AND ANNIVERSARIES

You put reminders in your diary, phone, or
your online calendar so that you remember
the momentous occasions that your friends
and loved ones celebrate. Even an e-mail that
acknowledges such a day is appreciated.

Empowering Affirmation . . .

I take the time to acknowledge my
friends' and loved ones' special days.

TREASURE YOUR FURRY AND FEATHERED FRIENDS

If your situation allows, you adopt a pet and give it a loving home. If this is not possible, you express love to all the animals on your path and treat them like the precious companions they have come to this planet to be.

Empowering Affirmation . . .

I love animals, and I express this love in any way I can.

SMILE OFTEN AND LOOK PEOPLE IN THE EYE

You meet people everywhere you go—those
you know and those who are new to you.
No matter who you meet, you smile,
shake hands if appropriate, and look them
in the eye when they are speaking.

Empowering Affirmation . . .

When I interact with others, I am
present, aware, and friendly.

PLAN FOR YOUR RETIREMENT

You plan ahead for your future, saving money
and discussing your plans with a financial
advisor if necessary. You don't assume that
the money will magically appear when you
retire. You know that, whatever your age,
you must take the necessary steps now.

Empowering Affirmation . . .

I plan my financial future now,
regardless of my current age.

LISTEN TO BOTH SIDES OF THE STORY AND DON'T JUDGE

One of the facts of life is that there are two sides to every story. You keep this in mind when assessing any issue, and you don't make decisions until you've heard and thought about both points of view.

Empowering Affirmation . . .

I listen to both sides of an issue before making any type of decision.

RESPECT PEOPLE'S BOUNDARIES

You are conscious of where to draw the line
when it comes to other people's boundaries
(as well as your own). When you sense that
someone is not comfortable with some type of
emotional or physical interaction, you back off.

Empowering Affirmation . . .

I respect people's boundaries by being
aware of what is appropriate and
what is not for each individual.

BROADEN YOUR HORIZONS THROUGH TRAVEL

You travel within your own country, as well as to faraway destinations, as a way of stimulating your mind, learning about other people, and just having fun!

Empowering Affirmation . . .

I travel both near and far as a way of broadening my horizons.

SPEAK WITH PROPER GRAMMAR

You know that there is a place for slang
and idiomatic expressions, but, for the
most part, you speak with proper grammar.
You represent yourself well by doing so,
and serve as an example to others.

Empowering Affirmation . . .

**I speak with proper grammar to
the best of my ability.**

MAINTAIN A HEALTHY BODY WEIGHT

You seek to maintain a body weight that is healthy and proportionate to your individual body type. Your body is your vehicle in this life, and you take care of it as you would a child.

Empowering Affirmation . . .

I accept my body and choose to fill it with nutritious foods and liquids, and to provide it with adequate rest. I love my body.

SEND LOVE TO
DIFFICULT INDIVIDUALS

Your so-called enemies are merely individuals
who are placed on your path as a way of teaching
you valuable lessons. You send these people love,
not hate, and positive energy is returned to you.

Empowering Affirmation . . .

**I send positive, rather than negative,
energy to those who challenge me.**

WRITE PERSONAL LETTERS

You take the time to actually handwrite letters, which you either mail or deliver to those in your life who have impacted you. This thoughtful act is appreciated.

Empowering Affirmation . . .

I compose and send letters as a way of expressing appreciation to special people in my life.

KEEP A JOURNAL OR DIARY

You keep a journal or diary as a way of getting
your thoughts and feelings on paper. Not
only does this improve your mental health,
but it's also a way to record significant events
that you might want to refer to years later.

Empowering Affirmation . . .

I write in a journal every day, and
find it very therapeutic.

ALLEVIATE STRESS

You find a way to deal with the stress in your
life by meditating, singing, saying affirmations,
practicing yoga, talking to friends, sitting quietly,
or doing anything else that works for you.

Empowering Affirmation . . .

**I engage in relaxing activities to
alleviate the stress in my life.**

RESPECT THE LAW

You do not pick and choose which laws
you abide by. You make yourself aware of
current and new laws, respect them, and
are proud of yourself for doing so.

Empowering Affirmation . . .

**I am a considerate citizen and serve
as an example to others.**

RESIST THE URGE TO JUDGE

You don't know what other people's personal situations are until you walk in their shoes, so you resist the temptation to judge others' actions, words, or physical appearance.

Empowering Affirmation . . .

I judge not, so that I will not be judged.

MIND YOUR OWN BUSINESS

You offer your opinion when asked; otherwise,
you mind your own business when it comes to
the affairs of others. You have enough on your
plate without interfering in other people's lives.

Empowering Affirmation . . .

**I tend to my own affairs and do not
interfere in those of others.**

LIVE FEARLESSLY

You live, love, and play without fear. You don't
want to reflect on your life years later and
wish you'd lived in a certain way, but you'd
held back because you were too afraid.

Empowering Affirmation . . .

I conduct my life fearlessly and proactively.

EMBRACE YOUR AGE

You celebrate each year of your life. You
are fully aware that your spirit does not
age, despite the passing of time.

Empowering Affirmation . . .

I am comfortable with myself at every age.

END RELATIONSHIPS
WITH SENSITIVITY

If you find that you have to sever a relationship
with a friend or a lover, you do so in the most
painless way possible. You do your best to
conduct yourself with honesty and compassion.

Empowering Affirmation . . .

I end relationships with empathy and compassion.

LEARN FROM YOUR MISTAKES

You don't continue to make the same mistakes over and over again. Rather, you learn something from every experience and make an effort to modify your behavior, so you are constantly growing and changing.

Empowering Affirmation...

I learn from my mistakes.
They allow me to grow and expand.

MAKE DECISIONS AND STICK TO THEM

You do whatever research you need to do before making any type of decision; but once you decide on something, you stick to your guns. You do not want to be regarded as someone who waffles back and forth and can't be counted on.

Empowering Affirmation . . .

I am decisive in all areas of my life.

TRUST YOUR INTUITION

You trust your intuition. You don't discount your
feelings when they tell you not to go somewhere,
date someone, or engage in some type of activity.
You listen attentively to your inner voice!

Empowering Affirmation . . .

**I listen to the voice that speaks
to me from within.**

LOVE YOUR BODY

You are grateful for your physical self, no matter what shape you're in. You love every part of your body. When someone gives you a compliment about your body, you say, "Thank you."

Empowering Affirmation . . .

I love and appreciate my body, from the top of my head to the tips of my toes.

SAY "I CAN" INSTEAD OF "I CAN'T"

You delete words such as *can't* from your
vocabulary. You can do anything you
put your mind to, so you use positive
terms such as *I can* and *I do*.

Empowering Affirmation . . .

I am a person of unlimited possibilities,
and my speech reflects this.

EXPLORE THE ART OF COOKING

You have the time and skill to cook a good
meal for yourself at least every now and then.
You choose an appealing recipe, buy fresh
ingredients, and make yourself a delicious meal.

Empowering Affirmation . . .

I view cooking as an expression of
love for myself and others.

PRACTICE FORGIVENESS

You know that forgiveness is something you do as much for yourself as for the other person. Forgiving doesn't mean necessarily condoning someone else's behavior; it's something you do for yourself to release resentment. Forgiveness sets you free.

Empowering Affirmation . . .

I practice forgiveness and free myself from all resentment.

ARE KIND TO EVERYONE YOU ENCOUNTER

Whether it's a homeless person on the corner,
a valet-parking attendant, or the queen, you are
friendly and polite to everyone you encounter.
You respect the fact that no one is beneath
you or above you—we are all human.

Empowering Affirmation . . .

I am kind and considerate to every
person who crosses my path.

ARE HUMBLE

Being humble is attractive. You acknowledge
your innate gifts, but do not boast about them
or seek to show off in front of others. You put
your talents to their best use by helping others.

Empowering Affirmation . . .

I am a confident, loving, and humble person.

RESPOND TO RUDENESS WITH KINDNESS

When you encounter someone who is rude
or inconsiderate, you respond with kindness
and tact. By doing the exact opposite of
what someone expects, sometimes you can
defuse the impolite behavior immediately.

Empowering Affirmation . . .

I turn the other cheek and refuse to
participate in rude behavior.

TAKE JOB HUNTING SERIOUSLY

You are meticulous when job hunting. You make
sure your résumé is in order and up-to-date,
and you do all you can to familiarize yourself
with prospective employers' businesses. Being
careless can mean the difference between
being called in for an interview . . . and not!

Empowering Affirmation . . .

I am meticulous when seeking employment.

PREPARE FOR THE INTERVIEW PROCESS

When you go to a job interview, you dress professionally; show up on time; and answer questions clearly, decisively, and respectfully. You research the company before you arrive, so you're prepared to answer any and all questions.

Empowering Affirmation . . .

I prepare carefully for job interviews and present myself as well as possible.

RESPECT YOUR EMPLOYER

You respect your employer by adhering to
company policies. You show up on time, offer
to help others, and work diligently. If your boss
points out a mistake, you say, "Thank you for
pointing that out. It won't happen again."

Empowering Affirmation . . .

I am an ideal employee and am rewarded
for my excellent performance.

MAKE YOUR HOME A BEAUTIFUL, PEACEFUL HAVEN

You decorate your living space in a way that
pleases you. The furniture, colors, floor and
wall coverings, and other accoutrements
that you choose reflect your personal
style and make you feel happy and calm
every time you enter your home.

Empowering Affirmation . . .

**I love my home, and I surround
myself with peace and beauty.**

PLAN A FUN DAY AND NIGHT

You take time out of your busy life to plan
an entire day where you have fun with
your friends and family. You might go on
a picnic, visit an amusement park, play
tennis, walk in the sunshine, go dancing,
or enjoy a delicious meal together.

Empowering Affirmation . . .

**I plan days where I can just have
fun with my loved ones.**

ACCENTUATE THE POSITIVE

You think positive thoughts, and your inner
(and outer) dialogue is a reflection of your
thinking. When a negative thought comes to
mind, you quickly replace it with a positive
one. Soon this becomes a way of life for you.

Empowering Affirmation . . .

I choose to think positive thoughts.

When you **Empower Yourself**, *you . . .*

ALLOW OTHERS TO TALK WITHOUT INTERRUPTING

Some people are waiting to talk, rarely allowing others to finish a sentence. You don't do this. You listen intently, wait until others are done speaking, and then reply.

Empowering Affirmation . . .

I listen while others are speaking and do not interrupt.

GET INVOLVED IN YOUR COMMUNITY

You take an active interest in your community. This may be by inviting your neighbors for a social gathering, offering to help an elderly citizen, volunteering at an animal shelter, or in another way.

Empowering Affirmation . . .

I take an active role in community affairs and reap the benefit of feeling engaged in society.

ATTEND TO YOUR STUDIES
WITH INTEGRITY

No matter what type or stage of schooling you're involved in, you are honest when it comes to taking tests and writing research papers. You treat other students and teachers with respect.

Empowering Affirmation . . .

I conduct myself honorably in
all scholastic situations.

KEEP LEARNING

You do not stop learning just because you're done with traditional schooling. You take adult-education and/or online classes, continually read new books and informative blogs, and attend lectures.

Empowering Affirmation . . .

I continue the learning process, even after I've graduated from high school or college.

ACT WITH CONFIDENCE

Sometimes you have to act like you have the
dream job, ideal lover, beautiful physique—
whatever. Once you are in the mind-set of
already having it . . . you attract the real thing!

Empowering Affirmation . . .

I am confident, successful, and joyous.

DREAM BIG

You dream the biggest dreams imaginable
because, as the Disney quote says, "If
you can dream it, you can do it." There
is nothing beyond your grasp, and you
place no limits on yourself with respect to
actions, deeds, or thoughts. You go for it!

Empowering Affirmation . . .

**I dream big dreams, and I
watch them materialize.**

SPEND TIME WITH CHILDREN

You spend time with children whenever
you can. By doing so, your own inner child
comes out to play, and you recapture the
innocence and freedom of your younger self.

Empowering Affirmation . . .

I spend time with children, and
I let my own inner child run free.

CAPTURE MEMORIES
WITH PHOTOS

You take pictures of friends, family members,
and special places and events, so that
you can keep these visual memories alive.
When you get older, you will be happy you
captured these special moments in time.

Empowering Affirmation . . .

**I capture magical moments to
keep special memories alive.**

SPEAK KINDLY

You avoid joining in when others are making disparaging comments about people behind their backs. You speak well of others.

Empowering Affirmation . . .

I speak kindly to myself and about others.

When you **Empower Yourself,** *you . . .*

CELEBRATE YOUR
NATURAL BEAUTY

You highlight your best features and let
your true beauty shine through.

Empowering Affirmation . . .

I allow my natural beauty to radiate.

When you **Empower Yourself***, you . . .*

WALK WITH CONFIDENCE

You walk with confidence—your back is
straight, and your gaze is forthright. Your
stance is a reflection of your inner self.

Empowering Affirmation . . .

**My good posture reflects my inner
power and confidence.**

ENGAGE EFFORTLESSLY
IN SOCIAL SITUATIONS

You are confident and comfortable when
mixing in groups, large or small, personal or
professional. You engage in conversation easily,
make new friends, and leave a good impression.

Empowering Affirmation . . .

**I am comfortable in small or large
groups and interact with ease.**

SAFEGUARD YOUR IDENTITY

You take care when using social media and
when sending texts or e-mails. You know that
the wrong people can sometimes get hold
of your information, so you do not divulge
personal details or send compromising
photos to those you can't trust.

Empowering Affirmation . . .

I am mindful when sending texts and
e-mails, and when using the Internet.

KEEP IN CONTACT WITH
LONG-STANDING FRIENDS

You continue to make new friends, but you
maintain long-standing relationships. You
make time to engage and connect again.

Empowering Affirmation . . .

I get in touch with someone from my past
and renew the friendship. I make time to
cultivate friendships, both old and new.

ACCEPT THE EMOTION OF GRIEF

There are times in life when you experience
grief—perhaps due to an illness, a death, a
breakup, or a lost opportunity—and that's natural.
You allow yourself to go through the stages of the
grieving process without guilt, shame, or regret.

Empowering Affirmation . . .

I allow myself to experience grief,
and I understand it's a journey
that will improve with time.

DO WHAT FEELS RIGHT

As you know, you can't please everyone. It's not important what other people think about you. As author Wayne Dyer once said: "What someone thinks about me is none of my business."

Empowering Affirmation . . .

I do what feels right for me and allow others their opinions.

SPEND WISELY

You respect your income. Whether
you prefer bargains or brand-name
labels, you budget accordingly.

Empowering Affirmation . . .

**I enjoy shopping but spend wisely
and within my budget.**

SPEAK UP!

When you're in a situation where you know you ought to say something—such as when someone makes an inappropriate remark and disrespects you or someone else—you say what needs to be said!

Empowering Affirmation . . .

I have the courage to speak up when necessary.

ARE TRUE TO YOURSELF

You remain true to yourself by standing up
for what you believe in, holding steadfast
when others challenge you, and adhering
to your morals. You live in your truth.

Empowering Affirmation . . .

I stand by my principles, even
in the face of opposition.

EMBRACE THE DIVINE

No matter what your faith, you believe that there is a force of good in the world. You know that there are times in your life when you need help, so call on the Divine and surrender.

Empowering Affirmation . . .

When I am overwhelmed, I embrace the Divine and know that I am supported.

STAY GROUNDED

You are practical, realistic, and sensible. You don't let the highs and lows of life affect you.

Empowering Affirmation . . .

I stay down-to-earth, even when things around me are chaotic.

BALANCE WORK AND PLAY

You work hard, but you also take time
each day for exercise, relaxation, and
socializing to maintain a healthy balance.

Empowering Affirmation . . .

**I work hard, but I make sure I have
an equal amount of fun!**

When you **Empower Yourself,** *you . . .*

ACCEPT CHANGE

Change is inevitable. But you accept it
as part of your evolution and understand
that it is happening for a reason.

Empowering Affirmation . . .

I embrace change as a natural process.

OPEN YOURSELF TO LOVING RELATIONSHIPS

Even if you may have been hurt in the past and are wary of entering into other relationships, you make an effort to open your heart and mind to accept and receive love.

Empowering Affirmation . . .

I open my heart and soul to allow love to flow.

LIVE IN THE MOMENT

You live in the here and now, in the present
moment. You realize that you are at your most
powerful when you are present while situations—
both postitive and negative—are unfolding.

Empowering Affirmation . . .

I am aware and present in every moment.

RECOGNIZE OPPORTUNITIES

You are open to the opportunities that present themselves to you, without doubt or feelings of unworthiness. You don't want to let life pass you by, or have regrets later on.

Empowering Affirmation . . .

I embrace the opportunities that I'm given.

RISE ABOVE PETTINESS

You are a substantial person with a strong
character and firmly held beliefs. When
others are acting petty and childish around
you, you do not stoop to their level. You
rise above it and move forward.

Empowering Affirmation . . .

I feel so much better when I rise above pettiness.

When you **Empower Yourself***, you . . .*

EXPRESS GENEROSITY

You are generous with your time, money,
and talents. It is just as important to
give as it is to receive. What you give
out really does come back to you.

Empowering Affirmation . . .

**I am generous to others, and I
receive so much good in return.**

MAINTAIN A PRACTICAL
VIEW OF SUCCESS

Your job and salary don't define you, as they can change in an instant. You are aware that success is a state of mind and comes from within.

Empowering Affirmation . . .

I am a success, regardless of my situation.

LIVE ORGANICALLY, AS MUCH AS POSSIBLE

You look for organic and cruelty-free produce and products when you can. You tread lightly on the planet and feel healthier as a result.

Empowering Affirmation . . .

**I choose to live organically,
when and where I can.**

*When you **Empower Yourself**, you . . .*

VALUE THE POWER OF TOUCH

Touching other beings is an essential part of
life, so you freely give physical attention to
those who are comfortable receiving it.

Empowering Affirmation . . .

**I value the power of touch—
both giving and receiving.**

When you **Empower Yourself***, you . . .*

EMBRACE YOUR INDIVIDUALITY

You are a unique individual, and no one in the
world is just like you. You do not have to conform
to anyone else's personal style or way of thinking.
You can just be *you*, in all your magnificence!

Empowering Affirmation . . .

**I celebrate my uniqueness and
individuality. I am happy to be me.**

When you **Empower Yourself***, you . . .*

CONSERVE ENERGY

You avoid waste and do your best to conserve
energy, water, and other resources that are vital
to this planet. You are conscious and aware!

Empowering Affirmation . . .

I respect and conserve Earth's precious resources.

VIEW OBSTACLES AS OPPORTUNITIES

If you are confronted by so-called challenges in your professional or personal life, you don't let them hold you back in any way. You deal with them and grow as a result.

Empowering Affirmation . . .

I view whatever is in my path as an opportunity for growth and expansion.

STRIVE FOR EXCELLENCE

You strive to do your best in every
endeavor you undertake, and you pride
yourself on your accomplishments.

Empowering Affirmation . . .

I strive for excellence in every situation.

STAY SANE

You have probably heard the saying,
"Insanity is doing the same thing over and
over again and expecting different results."
As such, when you do something wrong,
you acknowledge it and learn from it.

Empowering Affirmation . . .

I learn from my mistakes and move forward.

ASK FOR HELP WHEN YOU ARE FACING A CHALLENGE

You seek and accept offers of help when you are experiencing difficulty. We are all here to help each other through life's journey.

Empowering Affirmation . . .

I allow others to help me when I'm challenged.

SEEK THE BEAUTY WITHIN

You make assessments about others based on
the nature of their character and personality,
not their outward appearance. You know
that sometimes the best-looking people are
not so beautiful within, and vice versa.

Empowering Affirmation . . .

I see the beauty within others,
regardless of physical appearance.

LISTEN TO YOUR HEART

When making decisions about your love life, you
do what your heart tells you. You don't do what
you think you "should" do or what others tell you
to do . . . you do what truly feels *right* to you.

Empowering Affirmation . . .

I listen with love to my heart's messages.

ADAPT TO DIFFERENT SITUATIONS

You are at ease with people from all walks of
life, in both casual and professional arenas.
You feel comfortable no matter what you do.

Empowering Affirmation . . .

I adapt easily to different activities,
interactions, and individuals.

DONATE MONEY TO A WORTHY CAUSE

You donate to causes you're passionate about, when you're financially able. You know that even giving a small amount of money can do a lot of good.

Empowering Affirmation . . .

I donate to worthy causes whenever I can.

READ TO A CHILD OR
A SENIOR CITIZEN

You read to a child who cannot read yet, or
a senior citizen who is unable to do so. This
unselfish and caring act enriches both of you.

Empowering Affirmation . . .

**I enjoy the happiness it brings when I
read to those who are not able.**

MAINTAIN YOUR PHYSICAL HEALTH

You exercise regularly, maintain a healthy
weight, take vitamins, and eat nutritious foods.
Your vibrant health is the natural result!

Empowering Affirmation . . .

I do whatever I can to maintain optimal health.
My body is my temple, and I treat it as such.

MAKE YOUR OWN DECISIONS

You use your intuition and knowledge when you
need to deal with important issues. You might
consult with others during the preliminary
process, but the ultimate decision is up to you.

Empowering Affirmation . . .

I decide what is best for me in all situations.

SAY "I LOVE YOU"

You say "I love you" to friends and relatives. You don't assume that they know how you feel; you make sure to actually say those three little words!

Empowering Affirmation . . .

I tell the important people in my life that I love them.

START EACH DAY WITH
A GRATEFUL SMILE

You wake up with a smile each day, appreciating
your life, your health, your relationships,
and all the opportunities that await you.

Empowering Affirmation . . .

I smile when I wake up each day, expecting
the best and being grateful for all that I have.

REMEMBER THAT THIS, TOO, SHALL PASS

You know that no matter what happens, you can calmly deal with it, and it will eventually pass. Life is ever changing.

Empowering Affirmation . . .

I get through difficult times in a calm and realistic manner.

When you **Empower Yourself,** *you . . .*

VISUALIZE SUCCESS

You see yourself doing well in all areas
of your life: your job, your relationships,
your family interactions, your athletic
activities. The more you visualize, the more
success becomes a reality for you.

Empowering Affirmation . . .

I see myself succeeding in all my endeavors.

VALUE YOUR DREAMS

You find that by analyzing each person,
place, and thing that you dreamed about,
you can access important information
about yourself and your life.

Empowering Affirmation . . .

I remember my dreams and learn a
lot about myself through them.

FRESHEN UP YOUR LOOK

You mix up your style of clothing, your makeup,
and your hairstyle every now and then. When
you mix things up, you feel like a new you!

Empowering Affirmation . . .

**I update my personal style
to keep my look fresh.**

ARE A GOOD SPORT

You may be competitive when it comes
to games and athletics, but you play fair.
Win, lose, or draw, you're a good sport and
have kind words for your opponents.

Empowering Affirmation . . .

I compete fairly and maintain a good attitude.

THINK THE BEST OF OTHERS

People tend to assume that other people think
and act like they do. Since you are a good
person with a wonderful heart, you project that
onto others and it is reflected back on you.

Empowering Affirmation . . .

**I think the best of others, and
they think the best of me.**

WRITE WITH CARE

The words you write are a reflection of who you are. Whether you're writing a cover letter, an e-mail to a friend, or a personal note, you make sure you do so with care and consideration.

Empowering Affirmation . . .

I write with care and attention.

SETTLE DISPUTES CALMLY

You stay on an even keel when an issue arises
between you and another person. You don't
raise your voice and exacerbate the situation.
You remain composed, and state your case
in a clear and constructive manner.

Empowering Affirmation . . .

**I remain calm and reasonable
when involved in a dispute.**

RESPECT OTHERS' CUSTOMS

You've heard the expression "When in Rome . . ."
What this means is that you respect the traditions
of that place, even if they are unfamiliar to you.

Empowering Affirmation . . .

I respect the customs of those in other countries.

CELEBRATE THE MEMORIES OF THOSE WHO HAVE PASSED

You remember those who have passed
with love and appreciation. You recall
the good times and the laughter, and are
grateful for the times you shared.

Empowering Affirmation . . .

**When they pass, I celebrate the lives
of the people I have known.**

KEEP YOUR HOME AND OFFICE FREE OF CLUTTER

You feel so good when your living and
working environments are clean and
tidy. You feel at ease when your drawers,
closets, and files are organized.

Empowering Affirmation . . .

I make the time to keep things clean and
organized, as it helps me feel at ease.

ARE COURTEOUS AND RESPECTFUL TOWARD OTHER DRIVERS

If other drivers don't show you courtesy
on the road, you stay calm and choose to
let them pass, defusing the situation.

Empowering Affirmation . . .

I remain calm and concentrate on the road
ahead, showing respect to other drivers.

RESPECT THE IMAGE
YOU PROJECT

You are aware that your actions have
consequences, and can affect your image.
You think about the choices you make, being
mindful of the effect they can have.

Empowering Affirmation . . .

I make choices that reflect
positively on my image.

ATTRACT THE TEACHER WHO'S RIGHT FOR YOU

When you are open to new possibilities and are ready to learn, the right person will appear to guide you. You recognize your teacher when he or she appears, and you make the most of the experience.

Empowering Affirmation . . .

I attract the right teacher at the right time to guide me.

UNDERSTAND THAT YOUR ACTIONS HAVE POWER

You realize that every action has a reaction, so you consider the results of your actions—both large and small.

Empowering Affirmation . . .

I think before I act, knowing that the things I do have a flow-on effect.

STAY TRUE TO YOUR WORD

Whether you've committed to a new class,
hobby, athletic endeavor, relationship, or job,
you give it a chance if challenges arise.

Empowering Affirmation . . .

I live up to my personal and
professional commitments.

SURROUND YOURSELF
WITH POSITIVE PEOPLE

You associate with people who are kind,
compassionate, and joyous. You keep good
company, and you reflect these qualities yourself.

Empowering Affirmation ...

**I choose to be around people who uplift
and support me and themselves.**

ACKNOWLEDGE YOUR SELF-WORTH

You value yourself spiritually, mentally, and physically. You are a unique individual with so many talents and gifts. You look in the mirror and exclaim, "I am worthy!"

Empowering Affirmation . . .

I am worthy of all the good the world has to offer.

ACCEPT COMPLIMENTS GRACIOUSLY

You say a simple "thank you" when someone says something nice about you. You are worthy of praise and recognition!

Empowering Affirmation . . .

I accept compliments, as I know I am worthy of them.

VIEW EACH CHALLENGE
AS AN OPPORTUNITY

Contained in every "no" is a "yes" waiting
to happen. You know that when one
door closes, the Universe has something
even better in store for you.

Empowering Affirmation . . .

I know that every closed door means
another opportunity will arise. I believe
everything happens for a reason.

ARE RESPECTFUL OF
YOUR PRIVATE LIFE

It's okay to keep some things personal.
This is a way of respecting both yourself
and others who might be involved.

Empowering Affirmation . . .

I keep certain aspects of my life private.

LET YOUR PARENTS
BE THEMSELVES

You appreciate the fact that your mother and
father are humans who are doing the best
they can with their knowledge and skills.
You don't expect them to be perfect, and
they don't expect perfection from you.

Empowering Affirmation . . .

**I love and accept my parents for who they are
and know that they have the best intentions.**

When you Empower Yourself, you . . .

ARE A GOOD NEIGHBOR

You smile at and acknowledge your
neighbors. You find that all it takes to make
a neighbor a friend is a little respect.

I show respect for my neighbors,
and they show respect for me.

ARE TRUSTWORTHY

Your friends, relatives, and employers regard you
as someone who is honest and trustworthy.

Empowering Affirmation . . .

I am respectful of the confidences
people share with me.

ALLOW YOURSELF TO CRY

You let yourself shed tears when you
feel the need. You acknowledge that it's
not a sign of weakness—it's a freeing
act for your body, mind, and soul.

Empowering Affirmation . . .

**I cry when I need to,
as this is a good release.**

LAUGH OFTEN

You see the humor in everyday life and let
yourself laugh out loud on a regular basis.

Empowering Affirmation . . .

I enjoy expressing and sharing my
sense of humor, and I laugh often.

REACH OUT TO SOMEONE
UNEXPECTEDLY

You get in touch with someone you care
about for no particular reason, other than
to say you're thinking about them.

Empowering Affirmation . . .

**I maintain communication with others
without expecting anything in return.**

When you **Empower Yourself,** *you* . . .

HAVE HOPE

You trust that things will work out for the best and that your life will get better every day. Your belief keeps you going when things get rough.

Empowering Affirmation . . .

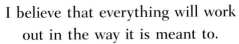

I believe that everything will work
out in the way it is meant to.

IDENTIFY YOUR PASSION

You trust yourself to look within and
acknowledge what you're truly passionate about.
You pursue this passion with enthusiasm.

Empowering Affirmation . . .

I discover my passion, and this uplifts me.

COMMUNICATE WITH YOURSELF

You communicate with yourself openly and
honestly. You note all the ways that you appreciate
you, and you express love for yourself.

Empowering Affirmation . . .

**I communicate with myself
often and with kindness.**

EXPAND YOUR VOCABULARY

You seek the meaning of words that you're not familiar with, rather than just skipping over them. And if someone uses a word in conversation that you don't know, you either ask or look it up later!

Empowering Affirmation . . .

I constantly take note of words
I've never used, to refine and improve
my communication with others.

When you Empower Yourself, you . . .

EXPAND YOUR MIND

Whenever a new concept presents itself,
you dig deeper to expand your knowledge
and broaden your outlook on life.

Empowering Affirmation . . .

I strive to expand my intellect with
fresh and innovative thoughts.

APPRECIATE WATER

You are mindful at all times when you
are using water, as you know it is one
of Earth's precious resources.

Empowering Affirmation . . .

**I respect and value the water that
is available to me and others.**

ENJOY A COMMITMENT-FREE DAY

You schedule a day where you don't "need
to" do anything or feel that you "have to" be
somewhere! You simply relax and enjoy!

Empowering Affirmation . . .

**I set aside time to simply
be in the moment.**

RELEASE PAINFUL MEMORIES

You let go of upsetting or challenging issues from your past and affirm that the present is your new reality. Today is a new beginning for you.

Empowering Affirmation . . .

I release painful memories and
move forward with joy.

ENJOY THE SUNSHINE

You go outside on sunny days and soak up
the soothing warmth in moderation. You
remember to wear a hat and sun protection.

Empowering Affirmation . . .

I let the sun's soothing rays wash over me.

ARE A MINDFUL TRAVELER

You pack your bag efficiently and give yourself
enough time to get to your destination, so that
your travel experience is a delightful one.

Empowering Affirmation . . .

**I carefully prepare for travel and
enjoy the experience.**

CELEBRATE YOUR BIRTHDAY

Your birthday is a day to rejoice, to get
together with friends and family, and to
express gratitude for the gift of life.

Empowering Affirmation . . .

I celebrate my birthday with joy.

When you **Empower Yourself,** *you . . .*

VISUALIZE YOUR DREAMS

You collect images that illustrate your goals
and dreams, and you use them to create
a collage. You look at this often, so that
your vision transforms into reality.

Empowering Affirmation . . .

I create a visual collage that represents my life
goals, and enjoy watching them come true!

ACCEPT GIFTS

When you receive a gift, accept it with
warmth and thanks. That's the best
way to express your gratitude.

Empowering Affirmation . . .

I receive all that is given to me with gratitude.

ARE AWARE OF THE THINGS YOU SAY TO YOURSELF

You notice the thoughts that go through your mind. You make sure these thoughts are positive. Thinking positively, on a continual basis, changes your life for the better.

Empowering Affirmation . . .

I choose positive thoughts.

EXPLORE NEW INTERESTS

You are continuously growing and expanding.
Every once in a while, you take up a
hobby that teaches you a new skill and
increases your interactions with others.

Empowering Affirmation . . .

I take up a new interest to enrich my life
experiences or explore something new.

RESPECT THE OPINIONS
OF OTHERS

You may not agree with other people's
views, but you respect their right to
have those opinions and understand that
everyone is entitled to their perspective.

Empowering Affirmation . . .

**I respect others' points of view, even if
they are different from my own.**

MAKE NATURE PART OF YOUR LIFE

Whether it's taking a walk in the park,
having a swim at the beach, sitting in a
garden, or reading a book under a tree,
you make time to connect with nature.

Empowering Affirmation . . .

**I connect to nature and feel grounded,
energized, and restored.**

SHARPEN YOUR MIND

You meditate, use affirmations, and visualize
what you want as a way of nurturing your mind.

Empowering Affirmation . . .

I take just as much care with my mental
health as I do with my physical health.

When you **Empower Yourself,** *you . . .*

ARE AWARE OF YOUR BREATH

You breathe consciously. You calmly inhale peace
and well-being, and then exhale any worries.

Empowering Affirmation . . .

**I remember to be present with my
breath as I go about my day.**

EMBRACE YOUR AUTHENTIC SELF

You are comfortable in your skin and
accept your strengths and weaknesses.
You are authentic and real.

Empowering Affirmation . . .

I am authentic in what I do and say.

EXERCISE PATIENCE

You are patient when dealing with others you encounter throughout the day. You accept that everyone doesn't move at the same pace you do.

Empowering Affirmation . . .

I am patient with myself and others.

EAT CONSCIOUSLY

When you eat, you savor each mouthful,
enjoying the flavors and textures. You eat in
moderation and stop when you're full. You
feel much better afterward when you do so!

Empowering Affirmation . . .

I enjoy and savor every mouthful.

TAKE A RELAXING BATH

Set aside time now and then to pamper
yourself by taking a soothing, relaxing
bath. You allow yourself to unwind in
the warmth and comfort of it.

Empowering Affirmation . . .

I soothe my body and soul by taking a bath.

ENJOY YOUR OWN COMPANY

You are your own best friend and you appreciate
your time alone. Your sense of well-being is
restored by quiet moments of reflection.

Empowering Affirmation . . .

**I enjoy my own company as much
as I enjoy being with others.**

CULTIVATE YOUR SPIRITUAL LIFE

Depending on your beliefs, you use prayer,
meditation, visualization, or chanting as a
way of connecting and centering yourself.
You are aware that you don't have to be
"religious" in order to be spiritual.

Empowering Affirmation . . .

I am a spiritual being with a strong
connection to the Divine.

STAY TRUE TO YOUR VALUES

You make up your mind based on your
own values and morals. You are not swayed
by the actions or opinions of others. You
are your own person, and you don't back
down when it comes to your beliefs.

Empowering Affirmation . . .

I stand by what I believe in.

CREATE GOOD KARMA

You live in a world of push and pull, cause and effect. You understand that what you put out comes back to you, so you create good karma through positive thoughts, actions, and energy.

Empowering Affirmation . . .

I respect the laws of cause and effect and live my life accordingly.

USE YOUR IMAGINATION

Your imagination is a creative tool of your mind
that can lead you to wondrous experiences.
When you let it soar, incredible things happen!

Empowering Affirmation . . .

**I use my imagination to create
wonderful experiences.**

TAKE REGULAR HOLIDAYS

Sometimes you just need a break, so you take
a vacation—or perhaps a *stay*-cation—where
you can just indulge in fun, entertaining
activities . . . and not do any work at all.

Empowering Affirmation . . .

I give myself a break from day-to-
day life by taking a holiday.

When you **Empower Yourself**, *you . . .*

ENJOY LIFE TO THE FULLEST

You're a positive, upbeat person who feels
appreciation and gratitude for your life.

Empowering Affirmation . . .

I enjoy life to the fullest and appreciate
what each moment brings.

BELIEVE THAT
ANYTHING IS POSSIBLE

You believe in limitless possibilities
and opportunities for happiness,
success, and abundance.

Empowering Affirmation . . .

I am open to all possibilities and
do not place limits on myself.

RELEASE UNHEALTHY FEELINGS

You admire others for their beauty, talents, skills,
and achievements. This shouldn't lead to jealousy
and resentment; although they are a part of life,
in the long run they accomplish nothing positive.

Empowering Affirmation . . .

I appreciate, rather than resent, the
attributes and talents of others.

OVERCOME YOUR FEARS

You seek out therapeutic ways to overcome your
fears, rather than just accepting them as lifelong
burdens that you have to live with. You *do* have
the inner strength to overcome anything you wish!

Empowering Affirmation . . .

I take positive steps to overcome my fears.

When you **Empower Yourself,** *you . . .*

PUT MATERIAL POSSESSIONS IN PERSPECTIVE

You enjoy what money can buy, but you don't obsess over material things. You don't judge others based on what they have.

Empowering Affirmation . . .

I value people over possessions.

DON'T ACCEPT ANY TYPE OF ABUSE

You don't tolerate being verbally, physically,
or emotionally abused by *anyone*.

Empowering Affirmation . . .

**I respect myself too much to
accept any type of abuse.**

TAKE CARE OF YOURSELF

You are a compassionate person who enjoys taking
care of people you love. You nurture yourself by
tending to your wants and needs, so that you
can care for others to the best of your ability.

Empowering Affirmation . . .

I take care of myself first, so that
I can give my best to others.

When you **Empower Yourself**, *you . . .*

GIVE THANKS FOR YOUR FOOD

You are thankful for every meal you eat. You
give thanks to everyone who participated
in putting food on your table, from those
who farmed and transported it, to those
who took the time to prepare it.

Empowering Affirmation . . .

I give thanks for the food I eat each day.

ADD MUSIC TO YOUR LIFE

You fill your home and surroundings
with the music you love. Music adds a
wonderful dimension to your life!

Empowering Affirmation . . .

I fill my life with the vibration of music.

ALLOW ADEQUATE TIME FOR SLEEP

Sleep allows your mind and body to rest and rejuvenate. Ensure that your resting environment is calm and tranquil.

Empowering Affirmation . . .

I prepare for a good night's rest, and I feel wonderfully energized when I wake.

When you **Empower Yourself,** *you . . .*

APPRECIATE YOUR FREEDOM

You're aware that there are places in the world
where people are not free, so you appreciate the
fact that you *are* free to vote, speak your mind,
travel wherever you wish, choose the career you
desire, own a home, be in the type of relationship
that makes you happy, and so much more!

Empowering Affirmation . . .

**I appreciate the freedoms I enjoy
in all areas of my life.**

KEEP YOURSELF HYDRATED

You drink a good amount of clean, fresh
water each day in order to hydrate your body,
eliminate toxins, and improve your overall
health. Your body is made up of roughly
75 percent water, so you replenish it.

Empowering Affirmation . . .

I drink enough water each day for optimal health.

AVOID UNCERTAINTY

You understand that some decisions
need to be thought through first. But
then, you take decisive action.

Empowering Affirmation . . .

I do what I need to do on time, and on purpose.

CREATE A TRUE PARTNERSHIP

Your relationship with your partner is a
loving partnership. It is one of mutual
respect and commitment, with a healthy
balance of yin and yang energies. This is
the foundation of a healthy relationship.

Empowering Affirmation . . .

**My relationship with my partner is
loving, balanced, and committed.**

USE YOUR INFLUENCE MINDFULLY

If you are in an influential position,
you are conscious of the effect your
actions and words can have. You act with
kindness and are respectful of others.

Empowering Affirmation . . .

**I use my influence in a positive way,
to bring out the best in others.**

When you **Empower Yourself***, you . . .*

STAY ACTIVE

No matter what the exercise, you find an activity that you enjoy and that gets your heart pumping. You aim to get your body moving for at least 30 minutes a day, to stay healthy and release emotions.

Empowering Affirmation . . .

I take every opportunity I can to exercise.

ONLY BUY WHAT YOU CAN AFFORD

You manage your finances in such a way that you have no need to borrow money from others or rely on credit cards. If you do need to use them at times, you pay them off in full at the end of the month to avoid finance charges.

Empowering Affirmation . . .

I manage my finances with common sense and good planning.

When you **Empower Yourself,** *you . . .*

ASSERT YOURSELF WHEN APPROPRIATE

You speak honestly and passionately about your feelings and aren't afraid of what others think. You are courteous and respectful, but you *do* get your point across.

Empowering Affirmation . . .

I assert myself when I need to.

FORGIVE YOURSELF

You may have done things you wish you hadn't, or said things you wish you could take back, but you know that there's no point in feeling guilty. Instead, you apologize to others if needed, forgive yourself, and do your best not to repeat these behaviors.

Empowering Affirmation . . .

I replace guilt with acceptance and forgiveness . . . and move forward.

LOOK AT THE BIG PICTURE

You avoid getting into arguments and disputes. Rather, you direct your emotional energy toward those things that really matter, and you let go of the small stuff.

Empowering Affirmation . . .

I choose to focus on what is really important rather than on small issues.

MAKE THINGS HAPPEN

You are proactive. You don't wait for other
people to create opportunities for you—*you*
are the one who makes things happen.

Empowering Affirmation . . .

I create my reality rather than waiting
for opportunities to arise.

When you **Empower Yourself,** *you . . .*

STAND UP TO BULLYING

You do something about it when someone is being bullied—whether it's a fellow student, a colleague, a stranger, or yourself. You let the bully know that this behavior is unacceptable, and, if necessary, you report the situation or seek help.

Empowering Affirmation . . .

I speak up when I see that someone is being bullied.

CREATE A SANCTUARY

You create a beautiful sanctuary in
your home where you can relax and
enjoy some personal time for you.

Empowering Affirmation . . .

I create a private, peaceful area in my home
where I can rejuvenate and restore.

ARE INTERESTED IN MANY TOPICS

You enjoy talking to diverse individuals
on a variety of subjects. You study, read,
and listen to expand your knowledge, so
you can have informed discussions.

Empowering Affirmation . . .

My mind is consistently open to new
and exciting topics and experiences.

DEVELOP FLEXIBILITY

You relax your rigid beliefs about how things in
your life are "supposed" to be, and you open
yourself up to more flexible viewpoints. When you
do so, you find that it's actually a relief to let go.

Empowering Affirmation . . .

I am flexible. I breathe, and just let go.

CREATE A CAREER YOU LOVE

You know that taking a job just for the money
doesn't make you happy, so you seek out a
career that fulfills you. You focus on what
you really want, attracting opportunities that
lead you in the direction you want to go.

Empowering Affirmation . . .

I love my job, and I feel productive every day.

When you **Empower Yourself,** *you . . .*

ARE INDEPENDENT

While you recognize that sometimes
you need assistance, you don't rely on
others for financial support, to tell you
how to live, or to "make" you happy.

Empowering Affirmation . . .

I depend on myself for the things
that I want and need.

CONNECT TO THE FLOW OF LIFE

You connect to the natural flow of life. When you do so, you encounter just the right people for your current situation, the necessary information appears on your path, and everything goes smoothly. You're in the flow!

Empowering Affirmation . . .

I am in the flow, and
all I need is available to me.

READ LABELS

You read labels on the foods and products
you buy so you know what you're putting in,
on, and around your body. When possible,
you support manufacturers that engage
in cruelty-free practices and contribute
to a safe and healthy environment.

I make sure I know what is in the
foods and products I buy, and support
manufacturers I respect.

When you **Empower Yourself,** *you . . .*

TAKE CONSCIOUS RISKS

You aren't afraid to try what is new and different.
When a situation arises where taking a risk
could help you move forward, you go for it!

Empowering Affirmation . . .

I take calculated risks and follow my passion.

WITNESS THE MAGIC OF THE UNIVERSE

You make every effort to take nothing for granted in your world. You appreciate the sun that rises and sets every day, the ebb and flow of the tides, the miracle of life, and the power of love. The Universe is truly magical!

Empowering Affirmation . . .

I appreciate the magical world I live in.

TREAT YOUR BODY LIKE A TEMPLE

You do your best to eat nutritious, healthy foods that are free of pesticides, additives, and artificial ingredients. You keep your sugar intake to a minimum and consume lots of fresh fruits and vegetables. You are in awe of your body—it is truly a miracle!

Empowering Affirmation . . .

I eat well, and my body serves me well in return.

ARE HAPPY IN OR OUT
OF A RELATIONSHIP

You are strong, powerful, and confident
whether or not you're in a relationship. You
realize that happiness comes from within,
and you appreciate your own company.

Empowering Affirmation . . .

I enjoy my time alone, and the sense
of peacefulness this brings.

GIVE ADVICE WHEN ASKED

You give advice when friends or family members ask for it, but you don't offer it if it's not requested. Instead, you listen to others with care, and respond appropriately.

Empowering Affirmation . . .

I give advice to others only when I am asked.

BOOST YOUR ENERGY LEVELS

Life can be busy and challenging at times,
so you refresh your mind and soul by doing
whatever it is that recharges your batteries.
Your body thanks you for your attention!

Empowering Affirmation . . .

**I recharge my body and mind
and feel invigorated.**

RELEASE UNREASONABLE EXPECTATIONS

Trying to predict how life will evolve can often lead to disappointment. You let go of expectations about how the different aspects of your life will play out, and instead let things progress naturally.

Empowering Affirmation . . .

I allow life to unfold naturally, and trust that everything is as it should be.

ACKNOWLEDGE LIFE'S LESSONS

You accept that the true meaning of a situation may not be clear at the time, but that in everything life brings, there is a lesson.

Empowering Affirmation . . .

I learn and grow, acknowledging and accepting all that happens.

BELIEVE IN YOUR
INNER STRENGTH

You draw on your inner strength during
difficult times and find that you can
handle just about anything. You are
strong, capable, and unflappable.

Empowering Affirmation . . .

I am strong and resilient and can handle
anything life puts in my path.

RELEASE ENERGY ZAPPERS FROM YOUR LIFE

You choose not to absorb negative energy from others. You gently release these individuals from your life and wish them well.

Empowering Affirmation . . .

I release those with negative energy from my life, in a gentle and loving way.

EXPRESS GRATITUDE
TO A MENTOR

You take the time to thank your mentors. You call, write, or e-mail them, and express your feelings of appreciation for what you've learned.

Empowering Affirmation . . .

I express appreciation to a mentor who has shared wisdom with me.

LOOK WITHIN FOR YOUR HAPPINESS

You don't look to other people to "make" you happy or "complete." You create your own joyous life with the choices you make, the actions you take, and the thoughts you think.

Empowering Affirmation . . .

I am already complete, and my happiness comes from within.

PERFORM UNSEEN
ACTS OF KINDNESS

You do something kind for a stranger and make their day. Perhaps you feed someone's parking meter, leave flowers on someone's doorstep, or donate anonymously to a charity.

Empowering Affirmation . . .

I show kindness without expectation.

*When you **Empower Yourself**, you . . .*

FEEL WORTHY OF ABUNDANCE

You are unique and deserving of good
things in all areas of your life. The
Universe provides for your every need.

Empowering Affirmation . . .

I am worthy of abundance.

ARE CONFIDENT

You walk, talk, and carry yourself with
confidence. This is one of your most
appealing characteristics, and your presence
is noticed by everyone who meets you.

Empowering Affirmation ...

I am a strong, powerful, and confident person!

When you **Empower Yourself,** *you . . .*

KNOW THAT WE ARE ALL UNIQUE

You are an amazing individual with unique
talents and abilities. You recognize these
qualities in everyone you meet.

Empowering Affirmation . . .

I value my special talents and those of others.

When you **Empower Yourself**, *you . . .*

USE POSITIVE WORDS TO EXPRESS YOURSELF

You eliminate negative words from your
vocabulary. Instead, you express yourself
by stating what you *do* like. You find
that you feel like a more positive person
when you speak . . . positively!

Empowering Affirmation . . .

I express myself by using positive words.

SOCIALIZE GRACEFULLY

You allow yourself to have fun and let loose with
your friends, being respectful of yourself and
others. You choose the right times and places
to party so you don't have regrets afterward.

Empowering Affirmation . . .

I socialize with my friends and enjoy my life.

When you **Empower Yourself,** *you . . .*

TAKE GOOD CARE OF YOUR SKIN

You nourish your skin like you do your body, using products that contain high-quality, nutrient-rich ingredients.

Empowering Affirmation . . .

My skin glows. It is clear and radiant.

LOVE YOURSELF

You love everything about yourself—
your mind, your body . . . your past, your future
. . . your essence, your spirit . . . everything!

Empowering Affirmation . . .

I love who I am . . . just the way I am.

ASSIST THOSE WHO CROSS YOUR PATH

You may not be able to save the world, but you *can* help those you encounter on your life's path. Whenever you have the opportunity to assist others, you do so.

Empowering Affirmation . . .

I make a positive impact on those who cross my path by helping where I can.

PRAISE YOURSELF FOR YOUR EFFORTS

You acknowledge the hard work you have put
in to maintain your body, mind, and spirit. You
promise yourself to keep growing and expanding.

Empowering Affirmation . . .

**I congratulate myself for continuing to
grow into a wonderful human being.**

CHOOSE YOUR
RELATIONSHIPS WITH CARE

You surround yourself with friends and loved ones
who are positive and supportive. You understand
that sometimes it's necessary to release people
from your life who have negative energy.
You do so with care and love . . .
and wish them well on their way.

Empowering Affirmation . . .

I surround myself with positive, loving,
supportive individuals.

*When you **Empower Yourself**, you . . .*

CONTINUE TO BE THE BEST *YOU* THAT YOU CAN BE!

You are the essence of beauty, love, success, and intelligence. You live life to the fullest and are grateful for every experience. You are a shining light on this wondrous planet!

Empowering Affirmation . . .

I am empowered—each day brings new and exciting experiences and opportunities!

A FEW FINAL WORDS . . .

Remember . . . you have the power within you to accomplish all of your dreams. No one can hold you back when you believe in yourself!

Know that you are loved and supported.

Much love,
Miranda
xxx

Louis Vuitton event in Sydney, Australia.

Backstage on *The Late Late Show with Craig Ferguson.*
It was such a fun interview.

On *The Ellen DeGeneres Show*. It was so special
when she told me she highly recommends
Treasure Yourself for young women.

One of my favorite designers, Alber Elbaz.
It was such an honor to walk the Lanvin show.

I love this Valentino dress. Orlando and I had
a great time together dancing the night
away at the *Vanity Fair* Oscar Party.

VOGUE

ITALIA

VISION OF FEMININITY

Vogue Italia shoot with my dog, Frankie.

British *Vogue* with Flynn.

Mum and Nan are two of the
strongest women I know.

Walking the runway for my friend
Stella McCartney's collection.

I am so proud to be associated with such
an iconic Australian brand, Qantas.

At the Met Ball in New York City.
It was such a great night.

Walking on set for Mango campaign.

Flynn and me baking muffins in the kitchen.

Mother's Day together 2013.

Having fun with Flynn, swinging around in NYC.

One of our favorite things to do together:
painting and drawing.

ACKNOWLEDGMENTS

There are many people who have made this book possible . . .

I would like to thank and acknowledge everyone at Hay House, especially Jill Kramer, Margie Tubbs, Rosie Barry, Dwayne Labbe, Rhett Nacson, and Leon Nacson, for making this book a reality.

I also would like to thank my family and friends, especially my son, who is the light of my life.

Finally, thank you to my team for your constant support.

To all who read this book . . .

Have the courage to speak your truth no matter how hard it can be.

Lots of love,
Miranda
xxx

ABOUT MIRANDA

Miranda Kerr was born and raised on a farm in Gunnedah, Australia. She began modeling after winning the *Dolly*/Impulse Modeling Competition in 1997. Although the win sparked significant media attention and she became the most sought-after new face, Miranda waited to begin modeling full-time until she had completed high school and trained in nutrition and health psychology.

Miranda's career has consisted of a mix of high-profile runway shows and fashion and beauty shoots, as well as advertising in television and print. Miranda was on the 3D cover of Italian *Vogue,* and she has also appeared on the cover of *Purple Fashion* and American *Elle.* She has been featured on the cover and inside of numerous magazines, including American, British, Russian, Spanish, Turkish, and Australian *Vogue;* American, British, and Australian *Harper's Bazaar; The New York Times' T Magazine; Numero; Jalouse; V; i-D; GQ; Love; Glamour;* and *Marie Claire.* She has worked with the industry's most renowned photographers, including Steven Meisel, Greg Kadel, Inez and Vinoodh, Patrick Demarchelier, Peter Lindbergh, Willy Vanderperre, Dan Jackson, Tom Munro, Terry Richardson, Alexei Hay, and Russell James.

In 2008, Victoria's Secret signed Miranda as its newest Angel. She was the first Australian model ever to appear in a Victoria's Secret runway show; in November 2011, at the Victoria's Secret Fashion Show, she modeled the iconic Fantasy Treasure Bra, worth US$2.5 million.

Miranda has walked the runway for designers such as Balenciaga, Stella McCartney, Miu Miu, Lanvin, Chanel, Prada, Christian Dior, John Galliano, and Loewe. Miranda has appeared in international luxury campaigns for Prada, Jil Sander, and Bally, and she worked with Reebok for their Easy Tone campaign. In 2012 Miranda was announced as the face of international fashion house Mango and Japanese handbag company Samantha Thavasa. Miranda is also the ambassador for Qantas Airlines and Kids Helpline.

Miranda is the founder and Managing Director of KORA Organics, her organic skin-care range. She is actively involved in the company on a daily basis. KORA Organics is currently available in over 400 stores in Australia and Japan, and internationally on www.koraorganics.com. KORA Organics also recently launched online with international luxury e-retailer Net-A-Porter.

In 2010, Miranda released her debut book, *Treasure Yourself,* with the aim of encouraging young women to embrace their individuality and listen to their hearts. *Treasure Yourself* has consistently been on the bestsellers list in Australia, and it has been translated into numerous languages. In 2011, Miranda was honored to have the book selected as part of the Australian Government's "Get Reading!" Initiative.

In early January 2011, Miranda and Orlando Bloom welcomed their baby boy, Flynn, into the world. When asked what her greatest achievement is to date, Miranda answers with true certainty: "Becoming a mother."

MIRANDA'S NETWORK

KORA Organics by Miranda Kerr: Miranda has personally created her own skin-care range KORA in conjunction with a team of organic skin-care experts. It's a range that she loves and uses every day. The quality of the ingredients is KORA's number one priority.

Miranda knows the success of her career is dependent upon her skin looking its best and in her remaining confident in her varying roles as one of the world's most sought-after supermodels.

KORA Organics provides that confidence, and it is the company's goal to inspire women of all ages to follow Miranda's lead to nurture their bodies, embrace their unique beauty, and understand the benefits of organic skin care.

KORA Organics contains pure essential oils and plant-derived and certified organic ingredients, and is enhanced with specific ingredients Miranda wanted in skin care for herself—all her knowledge of the tried and tested beauty secrets are contained in the KORA range.

Miranda and KORA Organics collectively strive to make a real and positive difference to people's skin.

"I have purposely added positive, loving words to every KORA skin-care product. Words like love, peace, empathy, *and* happiness, *so that these positive vibrations flow through to the products and on to the person using them."*

The range is available online from: www.koraorganics.com.

CHARITIES MIRANDA ACTIVELY SUPPORTS

Kids Helpline: www.kidshelp.com.au
Australian Koala Foundation: www.savethekoala.com

We hope you enjoyed this Hay House book. If you'd like
to receive our online catalog featuring additional information
on Hay House books and products, or if you'd like to find out more
about the Hay Foundation, please contact:

Hay House, Inc., P.O. Box 5100, Carlsbad, CA 92018-5100
(760) 431-7695 or (800) 654-5126
(760) 431-6948 (fax) or (800) 650-5115 (fax)
www.hayhouse.com® • www.hayfoundation.org

Published and distributed in Australia by: Hay House Australia Pty. Ltd.,
18/36 Ralph St., Alexandria NSW 2015 • *Phone:* 612-9669-4299
Fax: 612-9669-4144 • www.hayhouse.com.au

Published and distributed in the United Kingdom by: Hay House UK, Ltd.,
Astley House, 33 Notting Hill Gate, London W11 3JQ • *Phone:* 44-20-3675-2450
Fax: 44-20-3675-2451 • www.hayhouse.co.uk

Published and distributed in the Republic of South Africa by: Hay House
SA (Pty), Ltd., P.O. Box 990, Witkoppen 2068 • *Phone/Fax:* 27-11-467-8904
www.hayhouse.co.za

Published in India by: Hay House Publishers India, Muskaan Complex,
Plot No. 3, B-2, Vasant Kunj, New Delhi 110 070 • *Phone:* 91-11-4176-1620
Fax: 91-11-4176-1630 • www.hayhouse.co.in

Distributed in Canada by: Raincoast Books, 2440 Viking Way, Richmond, B.C.
V6V 1N2 • *Phone:* 1-800-663-5714 • *Fax:* 1-800-565-3770 • www.raincoast.com

Take Your Soul on a Vacation

Visit www.HealYourLife.com® to regroup, recharge, and
reconnect with your own magnificence. Featuring blogs, mind-body-spirit
news, and life-changing wisdom from Louise Hay and friends.

Visit www.HealYourLife.com today!